Character
What are you made of?

Sheila L. Johnson
Copyright © 2024 Sheila L. Johnson

All rights reserved.

All rights reserved. No part of the book may be reproduced, stored in a retrieval system, or transmitted in any form or by any means, including photocopying and recording, without the prior written permission from the author.

The information provided is for informational purposes and should not be considered a substitute for professional advice. The author disclaims any liability for any loss, damage, or disruption caused by the use of this material.

Cover by Adobe Express

Edited by Grammarly.com

DEDICATION

This book is dedicated to my grandson, Carmelo Johnson, and my granddaughter, Iyanna Johnson, who at the time of writing this book are under the age of four, and they will grow to be strong in character. That they will increase with wisdom, knowledge, and understanding of who Jesus is and that they will never depart from the faith that has been instilled in them.

CONTENTS

Chapter 1	Attentiveness	3
Chapter 2	Boldness	6
Chapter 3	Caution	8
Chapter 4	Diligent	11
Chapter 5	Forgiveness	15
Chapter 6	Grateful	18
Chapter 7	Hospitality	20
Chapter 8	Loyal	23
Chapter 9	Obedience	26
Chapter 10	Order	30
Chapter 11	Responsible	34
Chapter 12	Sensitive	37
Chapter 13	Trust	40
Chapter 14	Truth	45
Chapter 15	Virtue	50
Chapter 16	Wisdom	54
	Prayers	59
	Extra Notes	61

ACKNOWLEDGMENTS

I would like to thank the Lord Jesus Christ for the many blessings he has given me and my family over the years. It is because of my passion to help others to grow and develop in their relationship with Jesus and others that you are reading this material.

Many desire to learn the Word of God, but they are also unsure as too how to study or even where to begin. This workbook was written with you in mind. I pray that God will give you understanding and propel you to dive deeper into the Bible.

I thank God for my husband, Bruce of 33 years of his continual love and support who always encourages me to be better. I am so grateful unto the Lord for blessing me with 5 wonderful children, Mikeshaya "Shaya," Bruce Jr., and Bryan {Mikeshona and Yvonia, who have gone home to be with the Lord,} who are blessed and highly favored of the Lord. I thank God for overflowing my cup with two grandchildren, Carmelo and Iyanna, who have wisdom like Solomon and the Word of God is hidden in their hearts so they will never depart from it.

I thank God for every person who continually prays for me as I do God's will. I am especially thankful to God for you who have purchased this book. I pray that God will bless you abundantly, not just financially, but spiritually, emotionally, and mentally. I pray that you will always look to Jesus, who is your help, your shield, and your buckler.

INSTRUCTIONS

This workbook can be done alone or in a group. Each chapter is divinely written to help you in your personal growth and development as a Christian. In each study, the first step will always be to define the word being discussed. Use a Bible dictionary and a basic dictionary to define the word, allow it to light your direction through the scriptures and answer the remaining questions. A personal application is included for you to reflect on your new knowledge and identify areas for growth. At the end of the book you may add the area you need growth in along with a prayer

Prepare for God to open your understanding to his Word and give you a passion for more of Him.

HOW TO DO A WORD STUDY:

Materials needed: Dictionary, Greek and Hebrew Dictionary, Bible Dictionary, Writing Materials or Electronic Device.

1. Find a quiet place.
2. Be prepared to devote thirty minutes or more of uninterrupted time.
3. Begin with prayer, asking God to give you understanding.
4. Identify the word that you would like to learn about
5. Identify each place it is stated in the Bible, you can do this by looking at the back of your Bible in the index or your Bible Dictionary.
6. Locate the first place the word is stated in the Bible.
7. Define the meaning of the word in that scripture. If it is Old Testament look at the Hebrew definition, if it is New Testament look at the Greek definition.
8. You can also define the word in the basic dictionary to obtain more clarity.
9. Follow this same pattern until you have completed all the places the word is listed.
10. Compare to see if each place the word is used if it is the same definition. If there are different definitions consider putting the same one with the same meaning into a group.
11. Once you have the definition read it in place of the word in the scripture. In doing so this will allow you to gain clarity of what God is saying. When you have clarity you can apply it to your life. Ask the following questions: What did I learn about the word? How can I apply it to my life? What did I learn about Jesus?

TIP: When reading one scripture you may have to read above or below a few verses to get an understanding of what is being said.

CHAPTER 1 ~ ATTENTIVE

I am an introvert, meaning I may not be the one to initiate a conversation with someone, but I can communicate. I do not prefer the crowds, but I prefer a more intimate setting. The way that I refuel is by being alone. Although I am not a very talkative person, I am an effective listener. I am mindful of what the individual is saying as well as the way it is being said. I give the person my full attention, I am not fondling with my cell phone, or looking for items in my purse, rather, I am attentive to what they are saying. Although I am not a talkative person, when there is a matter in my heart that must be expressed I expect the person to give me their full attention. When a person does not, it sends signals in my mind that they don't care or what I am saying is not important to them. When I am talking and they begin to do other things, oftentimes I will end my conversation, I do this because I figure if they are interested they will pay attention, and since they are not I will save my energy. If you are an introvert you can relate.

My husband is the opposite, he is an extrovert, and he will talk to anyone who is in his path. However, he speaks with a purpose, to encourage individuals if they need it, to give and receive wisdom. He loves to be around people, it is his fuel. When we go to the store, in previous years my focus would be on what I came for, however, when we would go together, he would pay attention to the people walking, what was in their cart, the people that were standing around, what were they doing, the people in line what was in their hand. While he is looking he would be saying things like, "I should go help them lift that water" or "They might need a shopping cart with all that in their hand" he would always be attentive to others around him. After being married for thirty-three years, I began to be more attentive to people everywhere we went, if I would see a person struggling in any way, I would tell him and we would help if we could.

My husband's attentiveness allowed me to see how God is with us, he pays attention to every detail of our life, and even when we think He is not looking, He is. When He sees us struggling He will reach down {figuratively speaking} and help us, if we fall He will pick us up, when we are discouraged He has a way of encouraging us.

In **Psalms 130:2** the psalmist wanted God to be attentive to his prayer, we too should want the Lord to pay attention to us when we call out to Him in prayer. I take comfort in knowing that when I pray that God is listening, I never have to worry about Him not hearing me, or not understanding what I am going through, or what I need, He knows, He hears, and He will answer. The Lord also desire us to pay attention to Him when He is talking, He wants us to listen for every detail. Are you attentive to the voice of God?

STUDY QUESTIONS

1. Define Attentive.

   _____
   _____
   _____
   _____
   _____

2. Read *John 6:1-14* and note how Jesus gave attention to those individuals that followed him and write what you learn:

   _____
   _____
   _____
   _____
   _____
   _____
   _____
   _____

3. Read the following scriptures and write what you learn about being attentive:
   Philippians 2:4; First Corinthians 10:24; First Peter 3:8-9

   _____
   _____
   _____
   _____
   _____
   _____
   _____
   _____

4. One must be attentive to what the Lord is saying, read the following scriptures and write what you learn: *Luke 19:45-48; Nehemiah 8:2-3; Acts 16:14.*

_____
_____
_____
_____
_____
_____
_____

5. Read the following scriptures and see how when you pray, the Lord is attentive to your cry, and write what you learn. *Second Chronicles 6:40; Nehemiah 1:4-6, 11; Psalms 130:2.*

_____
_____
_____
_____
_____
_____
_____
_____
_____

EXTRA KNOWLEDGE: The word <u>attentive</u> is found 5 times in the Bible. Do a word study and see what God is saying.

Personal Application:

1. Make a conscious effort to pay attention to those individuals around you and ask the Lord how you might be of assistants to them.

2. When listening to a Sermon or Bible Study, silence your phone and take notes that you can go back and reflect on and apply to your life.

3. The next time you are in prayer, consider praying one of the above scriptures asking the Lord to be attentive to your cry, then make your petition known unto the Lord in faith, and finally pay attention to how he answers.

CHAPTER 2 ~ BOLDNESS

I come from a background where my mother was an alcoholic, this addiction brought with it many unhealthy behaviors. Growing up in this type of environment brought about many issues in my life, trust, anger, and low self-esteem. On many occasions, I could not express myself freely for fear of what others would say or think of me. I struggled with trust, due to my main caregiver, my mother, had broken it with her choices. My great-aunt was so gracious to care for me when my mother couldn't, which brought a sense of safety in my life. While I had a safe environment, it did not prevent the damage from my mother's behavior.

One day Jesus changed my life and the healing began, the girl who had no confidence now knew who she was, a child of God. The girl who was once concerned about what someone thought about her can boldly say that the Lord is her helper and she will not fear what a person may say or do.

Sometimes people are in situations where they need the courage to stand up for what is right. Fear grips the heart of losing what is familiar to them, and they remain silent. Three friends were commanded to do something contrary to their belief and if they refused they would be put in a burning fiery furnace. They never complied and were brought before leadership to give an account of their disobedience. The three friends boldly declared that they would not comply with his request and that the God that they serve would deliver them. The friends were delivered by God {*Daniel 3:1-30*}. What do you need to boldly stand up for?

When you surrender your life to the Lord Jesus Christ, He gives you the boldness to be who He created you to be and to say what He wants you to say. Have you been operating in fear and doubt about what God is telling you to do or say? As you go through this lesson take courage knowing that if God has asked you to do something He has equipped you with everything you need to fulfill the assignment.

STUDY QUESTIONS

1. Define Boldness.
   _____
   _____
   _____

2. Read *Proverbs 28:1* and tell how the righteous are.
   _____
   _____
   _____

3. As a child of God you have the right to come to God without fear or hesitating, read *Hebrews 4:15-16* and write what you learn.
   _____
   _____
   _____

4. It is your duty to declare God's business daily, read the following scriptures and write what you learn. *Acts 4:13; 9:26-30; 13:42-52; Ephesians 6:10-20; Hebrews 13:5-6*.
   _____
   _____
   _____
   _____

EXTRA KNOWLEDGE: The word <u>bold</u> is found 11 times, <u>boldly</u> 13 times, and <u>boldness</u> 10 times in the Bible. Do a word study and see what God is saying.

Personal Application:

Many people are bold, but they are bold in the wrong things. They do not hesitate to tell someone what is on their mind, but they are quiet when it comes to the things of God. As a child of the Most High God we must be bold for God. What can you do to boldly declare the things of God?

CHAPTER 3 ~ CAUTION

Growing up in Los Angeles, California there were so many things that a young person could get entangled in. When I wanted to go anywhere, to the movies with friends, outing on a Saturday night, or swimming at the park, my great-aunt, who raised me, would ask a multitude of questions, who was I going with? How was I getting there? What time was it over? Where is it? As a young person, I felt like I was old enough to take care of myself and that she was being too noisy. I didn't realize until I became an adult that she was showing her love and concern for my well-being.

Not only were there a multitude of questions, but I also had a curfew, a time in which I had to be back home. If it was a Saturday night event I had to be home by midnight. There were many times that I missed that time and came in after midnight, at first she would give me a warning that if this behavior kept repeating itself there would be some consequences. As a young person, I didn't pay any attention to the warning, because I thought I knew better than she did. Well, there came a time when I did not take heed of the warning and had to deal with the consequences. Some of the results of my disobedience were, not going outside for a length of time, maybe a couple of weeks, which in my days felt like years, or no talking on the phone, this was doing the time that there were no cell phones, this was downright devastating when my friends would call and ask to speak to me, they would hear, "Sheila can't have any phone calls". I had no one to blame, for the warning had been given.

God gives us warnings in his Word of things that we should not be doing and the consequences if we do them. He cautioned Adam and Eve not to eat from the tree of knowledge of good and evil, He was clear of what the consequences would be if they did. And just like me, they disobeyed and the consequences were detrimental{*Genesis 2:16-17; 3:1-3; Romans 5:12-19*}.

What has God given you warnings about, is it to separate yourself from a particular person or group of people? Is it from eating something? Is it from drinking something? What is causing you not to be obedient? As you go through this lesson determine that it is better to obey God and do what He says.

STUDY QUESTIONS

1. Define Caution.

2. Read *Exodus 23:13* and tell what one should be silent to.

3. Read the following scriptures and tell what a person should take heed to and why.
   Deuteronomy 4:9; Joshua 22:5, 23:11; Psalms 39:1; First Timothy 4:16

4. Read *Ephesians 5:15-21* and identify the warning{s}.

5. Read the following scriptures and write what one should be cautious of and why.
   Deuteronomy 6:10-25, 8:11-20; Matthew 7:15-16; Luke 12:15; Philippians 3:2; Colossians 2:8; Second Peter 3:9-18

   _____
   _____
   _____
   _____
   _____
   _____
   _____
   _____
   _____
   _____
   _____

6. Read ***Matthew 6:1-4*** and write what you learn about giving to those that are less fortune than you, such as the homeless.

   _____
   _____
   _____
   _____
   _____
   _____

EXTRA KNOWLEDGE: The phrase "take heed" is found 128 times in the Bible. Do a word study and see what God is saying.

Personal Application:

1. What do you need to be more cautious about doing?

2. What have you been warned to stop doing? And why haven't you obeyed?

3. Do you see the warning of Jesus coming are you prepared? If not, why?

CHAPTER 4 ~ DILIGENT

When I was in Middle school I began to realize that I had a love for becoming a beautician. I began scheduling clients, trying to build my clientele, but because I was just starting it was difficult. I would do a multiply of things, perms, press and curl, and braids, as I continued I realized that my passion was for braiding hair, I began to direct my attention there. In the beginning, what should have taken me a couple of hours would take me a couple of days. I had clients who would sit and get their hair done and promise to pay, only to suddenly disappear from the face of the earth. I had many days where I had no clients, but because I loved what I did, I would try to figure out a way to continue.

When I relocated from the Los Angeles area to the Inland Empire, this brought another challenge, no one knew me or the work that I did, I posted flyers in various places, and told everyone I came in contact with what I did. As I diligently did my part, advertising, and promoting through word of mouth, individuals began coming to get their hair braided. I had gained so many clients that I would be booked for months at a time. My clients did not get built in a day, but years.

When we come to God everything is new, we don't know how to pray or what to say. We don't know how we are to conduct ourselves as Christians, nor do we know what God requires of us, however, as we remain steadfast, unmovable, He shows us the way. He teaches us how to pray, as well as how He expects us to conduct ourselves as children of God. The way is not always easy and sometimes we become discouraged, as I did trying to build my clientele, but if we remain diligent there is a great reward waiting for us at the end.

What area do you find yourself discouraged in and want to quit? Is it unanswered prayers? Is it trying to stop a bad habit? As you go over the lesson find strength to not give in and quit, but to keep looking to Jesus for help.

STUDY QUESTIONS

1. Define Diligent.

2. Read *Proverbs 4:23* and write what you learn.

3. Read *Second Peter 1:5-8* and write what you learn.

4. Read *Second Peter 1:10* how does one make their calling and election sure?

5. Read *Second Peter 3:10-14* and write the rewards of being diligent about looking for the promises of God?

6. According to *Psalms 119:4* what are you commanded to do?

7. From *Psalms 119:4* define precepts.

8. According to *Joshua 22:5* what is your assignment?

9. According to *Proverbs 10:4* the diligent shall be made what?
_____

10. According to *Proverbs 12:27* the substance of the diligent is what and what does that mean?
_____
_____
_____

11. According to *Proverbs 13:4* what is the difference between the sluggard and the diligent?
_____
_____

12. According to *Proverbs 21:5* what does the thoughts of the diligent lead to?
_____
_____

13. Read *Second Corinthians 8:22* and see what others will do for a diligent person.
_____
_____

14. Read *Psalms 105:4* and see what is required in seeking the Lord.
_____
_____

15. According to *Hebrews 11:6* what will God do for the person who diligently seek him. Explain your answer.
_____
_____
_____

16. Read the following scriptures and write what you learn about receiving blessings.
    Deuteronomy 6:17-18, 11:13-25, Exodus 15:25-26; Isaiah 55:1-2
_____
_____
_____
_____
_____
_____

17. According to *Colossians 4:12* we should be diligent about praying for one another. Who needs help that you can pray for? List their name along with scriptures for what they need and then write a short prayer.

Example: Sheila Johnson for wisdom *First Kings 4:29*

Example Prayer: Dear Lord, I pray that you would bless Sheila Johnson with wisdom like you did Solomon, give her much wisdom and understanding according to *First Kings 4:29*. In Jesus Name!

_____
_____
_____
_____
_____
_____
_____
_____
_____
_____

EXTRA KNOWLEDGE: The word <u>diligent</u> is found 15 times, <u>diligence</u> is found 10 times in the Bible. Do a word study and see what God is saying.

Personal Application:

1. What have you been procrastinating about doing that you should be doing?

2. Are you diligent about searching yourself to ensure that you are in right standing with the Lord? If not, why?

CHAPTER 5 ~ FORGIVENESS

I previously mentioned that my background involved having an alcoholic mother whose behavior affected me, and how I was raised by my great-aunt. I didn't understand the choices that my mother made so I had a lot of questions, such as, why didn't she stop drinking and take care of me? I had trust issues and I knew it was because a healthy foundation was not laid. I needed healing from my past and the only way I could obtain it was to ask my mother those hard questions that remained in my heart and mind. When the opportunity came for me to have this discussion with her, I began with the first question and to see the look in my mothers face of the hurt that she had because of the choices that she made, I realized it was not worth it. As the days went by my mother began to express to me her childhood, she was not raised by her mother, which brought many questions in her heart. Some where along in her teenage years the door of alcohol got opened and it followed her for years. Listening to my mother I began to understand her upbringing and how things turned out the way that they did. Although I had an understanding of her past it did not neglect the hurt that I had, I had to make a choice, would I continue to hold on to what she did or would I release her? I choose to forgive her.

Forgiveness is a powerful thing that you have, it releases you to love again, to trust again, to find relationships again. We are imperfect people who are bound to hurt someone. We may offend them with something that we say or do. Most of the time it is not intentional, and we will need forgiveness. We have been instructed to forgive others so that we will be forgiven, {*Matthew 6:15*}.

We are all sinners in need of forgiveness, Jesus Christ died for our sin and if we come to Him and ask for forgiveness, He will forgive us and cleanse us from all unrighteousness, {*First John 1:9*}. And there is even more good news, after we come to Jesus and we do wrong, we can ask for forgiveness and He will forgive us and put us right back on the road to eternal life with Him, {*James 5:16*}. Have you asked for forgiveness from Jesus? If not, why? He is here for you waiting to forgive, there is nothing that you could have done or said that He will not forgive you.

STUDY QUESTIONS

1. Define Forgiveness.
   _____
   _____
   _____
   _____

2. *Matthew 6:9-15* Jesus gives us the pattern of prayer, read it and write what you learn about forgiveness.
   _____
   _____
   _____
   _____

3. Read *Matthew 18:15-22* and write what Jesus instructions are about forgiveness.
   _____
   _____
   _____
   _____

4. According to *Matthew 18:22* how often should you forgive a person. Explain your answer.
   _____
   _____
   _____
   _____

5. According to *Mark 11:25* when you pray you are also required to do what?
   _____
   _____
   _____
   _____

6. According to *Mark 11:25* what happens if you don't forgive a person?
   _____
   _____
   _____
   _____

7. According to *Luke 6:37* what happens when you forgive?
   _____
   _____
   _____
   _____

8. Read *Hebrews 12:15* and write what happens when you don't forgive.
_____
_____
_____

9. Define bitterness.
_____
_____
_____

10. Read the following scriptures and write what you learn about God's forgiveness.
    Second Chronicles 7:14; Psalms 86:5; Matthew 6:14; Mark 11:25-26; First John 1:9-10
_____
_____
_____
_____
_____
_____

EXTRA KNOWLEDGE: The word <u>forgive</u> is found 56 times, forgiveness is found 7 times in the Bible. Do a word study and see what God is saying.

Personal Application:

1. Is there someone that you need to forgive? If so, release that person today so that you can walk in God's freedom.

2. Forgiving someone is the beginning of your healing process, once you forgive them don't keep pressing the rewind button reminding them of what they did, instead press delete and start fresh.

3. Is there someone that you have done wrong that you need to ask for their forgiveness? If so, prepare you heart and do so.

CHAPTER 6 ~ GRATEFUL

God has blessed my husband and me with five children, three girls, and two boys. Fifteen years ago one of my daughters was attending college in Northern, California, and one was attending college in Atlanta, Georgia. The one in Georgia had come to California for a business trip and decided that she would go meet my daughter in Northern, California to attend a youth church service. She and my youngest daughter set out to meet her, however, they never made it due to a car accident. This was a very difficult time for my family, but God brought us through, and He is keeping us every day.

Many people ask me as the mother how can I be so strong or how do I make it everyday. My respond is always the same, I am grateful to God for his keeping power. You see my daughter Shona was going to take my other three children with her, my oldest son decided he didn't want to go and I thought my baby son would not enjoy himself surrounded by three girls, so my two sons didn't go, only my two daughters, Shona and Yvonia. God tells us to give Him thanks in all things, {*First Thessalonians 5:18*}. I am grateful that all my children did not pass, I am also grateful to God for allowing me fourteen years with Yvonia and twenty-one years with Shona.

It is easy to look at what we lose, a loved one, a job, or a house, however, when we keep on focusing on what we lost we never see or appreciate what we have or what we will receive. My three children are blessed and prosperous in their areas of life. God has also blessed me with two grandchildren. My granddaughter was named in honor of Yvonia and she was born on her birthday. God has a way of turning our sadness into joy, causing us to smile and be grateful.

When I look at my life there are so many things that I am grateful for, shelter, food, and family. I have learned not to take things or people for granted. I know that is your testimony also, you can look at the things that you have been through and where you are now and your hands are raised with adoration to God. As you do this study gain a deeper appreciation for what God has done for you.

STUDY QUESTIONS

1. Define grateful.
   _____
   _____
   _____

2. Read *Romans 1:18-32* and write what you learn when a person is unthankful.
   _____
   _____
   _____
   _____

3. Read *Second Kings 17:7-18* and write what you learn about the cause of the children of Israel sinning against God.
   _____
   _____
   _____
   _____

4. Read the following scriptures and see what, why, and how often one should give thanks unto God.
   Ephesians 5:20; Colossians 1:12; First Timothy 1:12 ; Hebrews 13:15
   _____
   _____
   _____
   _____

5. Read *Psalms 100:4* and tell how one should enter into church.
   _____
   _____

Personal Application:

Take some time to reflect on what God has done for you and what he is doing for you right now and give him thanks.

CHAPTER 7 ~ HOSPITALITY

My husband and I have been married for thirty-two years, when we first met I was a successful beautician, however, as the years passed and our family increased we decided that it would be best for me to become a stay at home mom, this meant that our finances would decrease. In a family of seven there were days that we had to get creative with our meals and some days we wondered what we would eat because the cabinets were bare. Our children never knew the struggle because every time we were low God would provide for us.

Having five children meant there would be five sets of friends and when the friends would visit this would mean snacks for everyone. Out of our five children, my baby son would bring the most people home, no matter how many times I would say, don't bring no one home with you today, they would always follow him. I would often wonder where the children parents were and why didn't they have to go straight home like our children. I later learned that most of them came from single-parent homes, who worked during the day.

When my children would come home from school they would come in like they hadn't eaten all day. Now imagine my baby son along with three or four of his friends coming in like they hadn't eaten all day. Although we didn't have much, I was always able to take what we had and feed the multitude. I had to learn more creative ways to stretch the food, sometimes I would take a can of biscuits and cut each one into four little pieces and make donuts with a cup of milk, or make pizza with English muffins. God always took the little that we had and stretched it allowing us to show hospitality to anyone that come to our home.

The Bible teaches us that we should be an example of Jesus and whatever we have we should be willing to share that with others. Being hospitable is not limited to how we treat guests in our home, but how we treat strangers also. If we want to be treated with kindness we should do the same.

STUDY QUESTIONS

1. Define hospitality.
   _____
   _____
   _____

2. Read *First Peter 4:9* and tell how one should use hospitality.
   _____
   _____

3. Read *Romans 12:9-18* and write what you learn about being hospitable.
   _____
   _____
   _____
   _____

4. From *Romans 12:9* define dissimulation and explain what love should be.
   _____
   _____
   _____
   _____

5. Read *Luke 14:12-14* and write what you learn about how we should treat strangers.
   _____
   _____
   _____
   _____

6. We should be wise in who we allow to come into our home, what are other ways that you can show hospitality when you make a meal?
   _____
   _____
   _____
   _____

7. Read *Luke 7:36-50* and write how a stranger/sinner treated Jesus in someone else home.

_____
_____
_____
_____

8. When you invite someone to your home how do you show hospitality?

_____
_____
_____
_____

9. From *Luke 7:36-50* write what happened to the woman that showed hospitality to Jesus.

_____
_____
_____

EXTRA KNOWLEDGE: The word <u>hospitality</u> is found 4 times in the Bible. Do a word study and see what God is saying.

> *Personal Application:*
>
> 1. How friendly are you to people when you are out shopping?
>
> 2. How thoughtful are you to others when it is not their birthday or holiday?
>
> 3. How do you show hospitality to your neighbors?

CHAPTER 8 ~ LOYAL

I sometimes teach a marriage class, and on one occasion I taught on how to handle the rough seasons. When couples go through difficult times there is the temptation to find companionship in someone else, but this is a breach in the contract or disloyalty to your spouse. The hurt of a spouse looking to someone else for physical or emotional comfort is heartbreaking. There is a saying that it is like adding fire to the flame, meaning one is already trying to handle the problems they are facing, be it financial problems or family matters, and to add infidelity brings more stress and pain. The couple should find support in each other, knowing that God will bring them through these difficult times. They should look to each other and God to bring them through. It is during the difficult season that they may need to draw closer to one another. They may have to cry together, pray together, and encourage each other, in order to make it out of the storm. This type of bonding during tough times will help to keep the couple in the days ahead. When they get the victory, they will be able to look back and say, "God brought us through."

When a couple make their vows before people and God, they promise to be there for one another, until death do them part. The same is true when a person come to Jesus, He is expecting us to remain loyal to Him. When trouble arises in a Christian's life, sometimes the easy route is to leave Jesus, stop praying, and stop fellowshipping with other believers, however, one should do the complete opposite, increase their prayer life, call your support group to pray for you, and remain with Jesus. Trials, difficult days, and challenging times are only for a season they will soon pass.

Others find themselves being loyal to a cause or the way something is done. While we do want to be faithful, when the cause becomes detrimental or the way of doing something is no longer working, one must be willing to make some changes. It is all right to let someone know that you will no longer be participating in what they are doing without giving a reason. It is all right to try to do something different, if it is for the better. Loyalty is important, but what or who you are loyal too is just as important. One's loyalty must be to Jesus and His cause, as you study the lesson exam yourself to make sure you are not unfaithful in any area.

STUDY QUESTIONS

1. Define loyal.

   _____
   _____
   _____

2. Some think that they cannot be faithful with little, they must wait until they have more to share, read *Luke 16:10-12* and write what you learn.

   _____
   _____
   _____

3. Some people don't want to be faithful in taking care of someone else belongings, such as the place they are renting or the job they are working on, even children living with their parents. Read *Luke 16:10-12* and see what happens when a person is not faithful in caring for another persons belongings and write what you learn.

   _____
   _____
   _____
   _____

4. Each one of us have been given something to do for God and the assignment is to remain faithful until he comes, read *Luke 19:11-26* and compare what each person did with what was given unto them.

   _____
   _____
   _____
   _____
   _____
   _____

5. According to *Luke 19:20* what did the person do with what was given unto him?

   _____
   _____

6. According to *Luke 19:21* what caused the person not to do anything?

   _____
   _____

7. According to *Luke 19:26* what happens to the person that is unfaithful.
   _____
   _____

8. Read *Revelation 2:10* and tell what will happen to the one that is faithful unto death.
   _____
   _____

9. Read *Matthew 24:45-51* and write what are the rewards of a faithful person.
   _____
   _____
   _____
   _____

10. Read *First Corinthians 4:17* and write what you learn about Timotheus.
    _____
    _____

11. Read *Numbers 12:1-10* and write what the Lord said about Moses.
    _____
    _____

12. Read the following scriptures and write what you learn about God.
    Deuteronomy 7:9; Psalms 36:5; Lamentations 3:22-23; Second Thessalonians 2:13; 3:3
    _____
    _____
    _____

EXTRA KNOWLEDGE: The word <u>faithful</u> is found 82 times in the Bible. Do a word study and see what God is saying.

> *Personal Application:*
>
> Are you the type of person that keep your word? Are you loyal to God and what he has called you to do? If not, take some time to see why not. Once you have identified the problem correct it and become a faithful person in all area.

CHAPTER 9 ~ OBEDIENCE

When I was growing up there were rules that I had to comply with living with my great aunt, and one of those rules was you had to do your chores before you could go outside. I know in today's time not very many children go outside, but during my days going outside was where you could find your friends and many activities. My obedience would allow me to participate.

As my husband and I began to establish our family we had to teach our children the importance of obedience, as I am sure if you have children you do or had to do the same. However, obedience is not just limited to children, it is required in everyone. Now let's be clear, one does not have to be obedient to anything that will cause harm or danger.

When I read the Bible there are certain things that God does automatically, the air we breathe, or the physical body working properly, but there are other things that require obedience in order to receive what is promised. As we look at this study exam to see if you are missing some of God's promises because of disobedience. If so, repent and get on the right road to obedience.

STUDY QUESTIONS

1. Define obedience.

2. Read *Romans 6:1-23* and write what you learn about obedience.

3. Read *Deuteronomy 13:4* and write what the instructions are.

4. Read *Acts 5:29* and write what Peter and the other apostles said.

5. Go back and read *Acts 5:17-28* and write why Peter and the other apostles said what they said.

6. Read *First Peter 2:13-17* and write what the instructions are.

7. Read *Luke 2:41-52* and write what did Jesus do to his parents in verse *51*.

8. According to *Luke 2:52* what did Jesus increase in?

9. Read *Deuteronomy 28:2-14* and write some of the promises for the obedient.

10. Read *Deuteronomy 28:15-68* and write some of the consequences of the disobedient.

11. Read *Exodus 23:22* and write what happens when you obey the voice of God.
   _____
   _____
   _____

12. Read *Luke 4:46-49* and write what you learn about obedience.
   _____
   _____
   _____
   _____

13. Read *Matthew 7:21-23* and write what the promise is to those that obey God.
   _____
   _____
   _____

14. According to *First Samuel 15:22* obedience is better than what?
   _____
   _____

15. Read *Proverbs 6:20-22* and write what you learn when a person obey the Word of God.
   _____
   _____
   _____

16. According to *Proverbs 6:21* how can a person obey the Word of God?
   _____
   _____
   _____

EXTRA KNOWLEDGE: The word <u>obey</u> is found 69 times, <u>obedience</u> is found 12 times in the Bible. Do a word study and see what God is saying.

Personal Application:

There are many things that God has given instructions in, how to live a Christian life, for example, do a Bible Study and find out what does require of you and then apply it.

CHAPTER 10 ~ ORDER

My husband and I had five children, three girls and two boys. With five children, a house can get a little chaotic. Because I was a stay-at-home mother I had to establish some order in my home if I wanted to maintain my sanity. Our day had to be strategically arranged, which included their meals, chores, study time, outside playing, and of course a nap. Because they were on a time schedule when it was nap time I could take this time to do the things that were necessary for me or my husband. If there was no order in my home I would not have been able to accomplished anything.

Some parents do not set order in their home and this causes them to become stressed or always in overload. Setting a schedule in your home will teach children how to be strategic and set order in their lives, it will also allow one to have consistency and a clear mind.

Everything has some type of order in it, schools, government, workplace, etc. Without order things would be chaotic. We find God setting order in the very beginning. He created the heaven and the earth and put things in their proper place with instructions.

God gave Moses directions to build a tabernacle and because He likes order He gave him every detail, from the order of the furniture, to who should have the position of offering up the sacrifices unto Him, {see the book of Exodus for complete details}. This was done for a pattern of things to come. In other words, God set up order for and in the Tabernacle to prepare us on how to maintain order in the church.

God has also given us directions as to how to have order in our lives, as you do this study, exam yourself and make sure that you are following God's way in everything that you do. If you are not sure how something should be done and it is not covered in this lesson, consider doing a Bible Study and get the information. Once you obtain the information make sure to apply it and help someone else.

STUDY QUESTIONS

1. Define order.
   _____
   _____
   _____

2. Read *First Corinthians 14:40* and write what you learn.
   _____
   _____

3. Read *Psalms 119:133* and write how God will direct you daily.
   _____
   _____

4. Read the following scriptures and write God's order for the married.
   Genesis 3:16; First Corinthians 11:3; Ephesians 5:23
   _____
   _____
   _____
   _____

5. Read the following scriptures and write what is the responsibility of the husband.
   Ephesians 5:25, 28; Colossians 3:19; First Peter 3:7; First Timothy 3:5
   _____
   _____
   _____
   _____
   _____
   _____

6. Read the following scriptures and write what is the responsibility of the wife.
   First Corinthians 7:34; Ephesians 5:22, 24, 33; First Peter 3:1-6
   _____
   _____
   _____
   _____
   _____
   _____

7. Based on what you have learned from questions 5 and 6 summarize why so many people divorce when things are out of order in the home.

___

8. Read the following scriptures and write what is the responsibility of children.
   Ephesians 6:1; Colossians 3:20

___

9. Based on what you have learned thus far summarize God's order for the home.

___

10. Read the following scriptures and write who is the head of the church.
    Ephesians 1:22-23, 5:23-24; Colossians 1:18

___

11. Read the following scriptures and write who did God place as the overseer of the church.
    Jeremiah 3:15, 23:1-2; Ephesians 4:11; First Peter 5:1-3; Acts 20:17-28

___

12. Read the following scriptures and write what the assignment is for others in the church.
    Exodus 18:13-26; Numbers 11:10-17; Acts 6:1-3

    _____
    _____
    _____
    _____
    _____
    _____

13. Read ***First Corinthians 14:33*** and write what God is not and explain your answer.

    _____
    _____
    _____
    _____
    _____

EXTRA KNOWLEDGE: The word <u>order</u> is found 61 times in the Bible. Do a word study and see what God is saying.

Personal Application:

1. God set the order in the beginning with Adam and Eve for the household, if you are married is your house in order, if not what can you do to get it in order?

2. The church must have order to maintain it, when things are out of order one could miss the move of God. Is there anything that you can do to help your church maintain order?

3. Is there something out of order in your relationship with Jesus, if so when are you going to get it in order?

CHAPTER 11 ~ RESPONSIBLE

I remember a time growing up in my teenage years when I was old enough to drive. I could not wait to have a car to be able to go wherever I wanted to go. I would ask my cousins if I could use their car, and of course the answer was always the same, no. One relative finally let me drive her car, she gave me the time I needed to have it back so that she could go to work. Oh the joy I felt, I began picking out my outfit and where I was going to go, I wanted all my friends to see that I knew how to drive and I was out on my own. I picked up the car from her house and headed back home to get ready for the evening. I was almost home when I heard a popping sound, a novice to driving on my own, I had no idea what it was, until I felt the car driving uneven on the road, that's when I realized I had a flat tire. I had never been in the car with anyone that had a flat drive, so I had no idea as to what to do. I pulled over on the side of the road and found a phone booth {no cell phones yet} to call my cousin to tell her. After I told her what happened, she reminded me what time she had to be at work at left the rest up to me. Well, that did not go the way I expected, I thought she was going to come and fix the tire and let me continue on with my evening. Since I was so close to home I called my cousin and asked him what should I do, he came and helped me and got the car back going, at my expense for the repairs. That put a change in my plans for the evening, I had the car and the outfit, but the funds were low due to unforeseen emergency.

That incident taught me to be responsible, that when you borrow someones things you are responsible for any damage that occur. We are not only responsible for repairing what we have broken, but we must be held accountable for our choices and actions. I cannot give an account for how someone else acts, I must give an account for how I act. I cannot give an account for what someone else says, I can only give an account for my words.

As a mother I am responsible for taking care of my children, training them in the direction that they should go, teaching them good manners, financial principles, and about God. I cannot leave this responsibility to anyone else. As a wife I am responsible for ministering to my husband, making sure that his needs are being met. As a Christian, I am responsible for learning what God says and applying it to my life. What are you responsible for? As you do this short study let's grow together.

STUDY QUESTIONS

1. Define responsible.
   _____
   _____
   _____

2. Read *John 21:20-23* and write what Jesus tells Peter that is also applicable to us.
   _____
   _____

3. Read *Jeremiah 17:10* and write who searches the heart and what will they give to everyone.
   _____
   _____

4. Read *Second Corinthians 5:10* and tell what everyone must do.
   _____
   _____

5. Read *Matthew 16:27* and tell who will be rewarded and what they will be rewarded for.
   _____
   _____

6. According to *Matthew 12:36* what must you give account for?
   _____
   _____

7. According to *Romans 14:12* who must give an account to God?
   _____
   _____

8. According to *Romans 14:13* you are responsible for what?
   _____
   _____

9. Read *Proverbs 22:6* and tell the responsibility of parents.
   _____
   _____
   _____

10. Read *Ephesians 6:4* and tell the responsibility of the fathers.

_____
_____

11. Read the following scriptures and tell the responsibility of husbands.
    Ephesians 5:25; Colossians 3:19; First Peter 3:7

_____
_____
_____

12. Read the following scriptures and tell the responsibility of wives.
    Ephesians 5:22, 24; Colossians 3:18; First Peter 3:1

_____
_____
_____

13. Read *First Corinthians 7:34* and tell the responsibility of those that are unmarried.

_____
_____

14. Read *Luke 12:35-48* and tell what will happen to the person that is irresponsible.

_____
_____

15. Read *Ezekiel 18:20* and tell who is responsible for the wrong that they do.

_____
_____

EXTRA KNOWLEDGE: The word <u>account</u> is found 17 times in the Bible. Do a word study and see what God is saying.

> *Personal Application:*
>
> You are responsible for what you do and say how can you grow in both?

CHAPTER 12 ~ SENSITIVE

Most days I am able to recognize my emotions, when I am stressed or hurting, and I am able to identify what is the cause. I can determine that I may be stressed because I am trying to solve a problem and can't find a solution. If the weather is nice I may take a brisk walk to release the stress or sing a song. Then there are days that I feel like I can't stop crying because I am so sensitive, I will let my husband know how I am feeling. Why do I tell him? Because he is my covering, therefore I know that he will cover me with prayer, but he will also shelter me from the harm that may come from those who don't know what I am experiencing. I will also let him know that I just need to be under him and a little more love. He will readjust his schedule and minister to me by staying close to me, holding me when necessary, he will be careful about when and how he speaks, when he does his words will always be saturated in love.

But there are other times when I am sensitive and it has nothing to do with me. During these days I will begin praying asking the Lord what is going on, because I have learned through the years that God will sometimes allow me to feel someones hurt or burden. Sometimes God will allow me to know who it is through prayer, for the Spirit of God knows how to intercede, their name will come to my mind and I will just pray as God leads. Usually, when this occurs he lifts it off of me when I pray, then there are other times where the weight will remain there for days and all I can do is stay sensitive for the voice of God to lead me as to what to do. Am I to continue to pray for them? Does he want me to call them? I have to stay sensitive to his voice.

The question may be asked how can I tell the difference between my feelings and a burden for someone else? The answer is God will always let me know the difference. Every Christian should have a prayer life. Prayer is communication between the individual and God. Prayer is our relationship with God, we talk He listens, He talks we listen. God doesn't just talk when we are in prayer, but when we are going about our everyday business, just as we don't just talk to God in our prayer time, but we talk to Him when we are driving, at work, and every where we go. This relationship allows you to be sensitive to his voice, like a mother sensitive to her child's voice. As you study this lesson ask God to give you ears to hear and eyes to see in the Spirit.

STUDY QUESTIONS

1. Define sensitive.
   _____
   _____
   _____

2. Read *Genesis 6:1-7:7* and write who was sensitive to the voice of the Lord.
   _____

3. From your above answer and *Genesis 6:1-7:7* describe what God told the person.
   _____
   _____
   _____
   _____
   _____
   _____
   _____
   _____

4. Read *Genesis 7:8-8:20* and write what happened because of the obedience of the person you named in question 2.
   _____
   _____
   _____
   _____
   _____
   _____

5. Read *Exodus 3:1-4* and write who was sensitive to the voice of the Lord.
   _____

6. Read *Exodus 4:27* and write who was sensitive to the voice of the Lord.
   _____

7. Read *Joshua 3:7* and write who was sensitive to the voice of the Lord.
   _____

8. Read *Acts 13:1-2* and tell who ministered and fasted to the Lord and what happened.

9. From *Acts 13:2* what caused them to be sensitive to the Holy Ghost?

10. Read *John 14:16-26* and write what you learn about the Comforter.

11. Read *First Kings 19:1-13* and summarize what you learn about Elijah and the voice of God.

Personal Application:

1. Are you able to recognize the voice of the Lord?

2. If not, how much time do you spend in prayer?

3. If you are able to recognize the voice the Lord are you quick to obey? If not why?

CHAPTER 13 ~ TRUST

In any relationship trust is a major factor. Individuals want to know that when they confine in you that their business will not be shared with others, that they can trust you. With so many television shows portraying men and women as cheaters, individuals are unsure if they should make long-term commitments, wondering will the person be devoted to them until death do them part. Programs that show friends betraying friends, many people are coming to the conclusion that there are no good people.

If you are like me your trust may have been broken many times, individuals promising to be there for you have not been able to keep their word. My first foundation of trust was broken by my primary caregiver, my mother, God allowed her to bring me in the world with the responsibility to nurture and care for me. Because of her addictions she was unable to do that, that laid the foundation for future relationships, that they were not to be trusted. This lie had to be broken. God began destroying that lie long before I came to Jesus. He did this by allowing my great-aunt to take me in and care for me, no matter how rebellious I was she would always correct me and not throw me away.

When I gave my life to Jesus, He began to show me the issue I had with trust and through his Word He began to break that lie and show me that He could be trusted, that He would always be there. He also began to show me how I could trust others also. Perhaps you were like me and your trust has been broken and you need God to restore it, as you study this lesson ask God to rebuild what was destroyed and learn that everyone is not the same, there are some people who have your best interest at heart, but most of all learn to trust God.

STUDY QUESTIONS

1. Define trust.

2. Read *Psalms 37:5* and describe what you should give to the Lord and what will happen.

3. Read *Psalms 40:4* and describe the person that trust the Lord.

4. Read the following scriptures and tell what a person should do when they are facing fear.
   Psalms 56:3-4, 11

5. Read *Psalms 62:8* and tell when should you trust God.

6. Read *Psalms 115:11* and tell what the Lord is to those that trust in him.

7. *Psalms 118:8-9* says that it is better to trust in the Lord than what or who?

8. Read *Proverbs 3:5* and describe how you should trust in the Lord.

_____
_____
_____

9. According to *Proverbs 29:25* what happens to those that trust in the Lord?

_____
_____
_____

10. According to *Jeremiah 7:4, 8* what should you not trust in and why?

_____
_____
_____

11. Read *Proverbs 25:19* and tell what it is like to trust in an unfaithful person.

_____
_____
_____

12. Read *Psalms 34:18* and describe who is close to them when they are broken or hurting.

_____
_____
_____

13. Read *Psalms 147:3* and describe what happens to a person whose trust has been broken.

_____
_____
_____

14. Read *Proverbs 11:13* and tell who can and cannot be trusted.

_____
_____
_____
_____

15. From *Proverbs 11:13* define a talebearer.

___

16. According to *Proverbs 17:9* who seeks love and the one that betrays your confidence does what?

___

17. Read *Proverbs 20:19* and write the words of wisdom.

___

18. Read *Proverbs 17:17* and describe a true friend.

___

19. Read *Ephesians 4:32* and tell what you should do to those that have done you wrong.

___

20. Forgiveness does not mean that you have forgotten, describe what happens when you forgive someone and how you can learn to trust again.

___

21. Read *Psalms 28:7* and write what the Psalmist said when he trusted in the Lord.

_____
_____
_____
_____

EXTRA KNOWLEDGE: The word <u>trust</u> is found 134 times and the word <u>trusted</u> is found 29 times in the Bible. Do a word study and see what God is saying.

Personal Application:

1. Is there someone that you need to forgive so that you can trust again? If so, what is preventing you from getting victory?

2. When we have been wounded we have to learn to trust again, what are ways that you can begin the process?

3. Is there an area that you have not learned to trust the Lord in yet? {Example: With your marriage? With your children? With your finances?} How can you learn to trust God in that area?

4. Trust is something that must be earned, look over your life and take note of areas where God has come through for you and be encouraged to know that if God did it before, He will do it again.

CHAPTER 14 ~ TRUTH

Truth what is it? With many lies being told it may seem hard to recognize it. Adam and Eve had been given instructions to freely eat from every tree in the garden except one. The instructions were that if they ate from that tree they would surely die. They did fine until Eve began holding a conversation with the serpent, as they conversed, she rehearsed to him the instructions that was given, the serpent, who was very cunning, added one little word, "not," that caused her to believe a lie. She and her husband ate from the forbidden tree and they died. This death was not a natural death, for they were able to sew figs leaves and make an outfit and continue to talk to one another. This was a spiritual death. We know this because God made a covering that was acceptable, coats of skins. The choice that Adam made has impacted the entire world, spiritual death has been passed down. The good news is Jesus Christ made a covering that is acceptable for the world, his death, burial, and resurrection. {See **Genesis 1-3; Romans 5**}

In the current time 2024, there are many preachers, prophets, and teachers that are proclaiming to be sent from God, how is one able to know who is teaching truth and who is not? The Bible gives us many clues to recognize a person who is not from God, as you do this study equip yourself so you decipher the difference.

STUDY QUESTIONS

1. Define truth.
   _____
   _____
   _____

2. Read *John 17:17* and tell what is truth.
   _____
   _____

3. Read the following scriptures and see if they confirm what *John 17:17* is saying and write what you learn.
   Psalms 12:6; 119:151, 160
   _____
   _____
   _____
   _____

4. Read *Isaiah 28:9-10* and write what you learn.
   _____
   _____
   _____

5. From *Isaiah 28:10* define precept.
   _____
   _____
   _____

6. Read *Matthew 7:15-20* and tell what you should beware of, and describe them.
   _____
   _____
   _____
   _____

7. Read *Matthew 24:3-24* and tell what is the first warning that Jesus gave.
   _____
   _____
   _____

8. Read *Matthew 24:5* and tell how many will come saying they are Christ.

9. Read *Matthew 24:11* and tell who will rise and how many.

10. Read *Matthew 24:24* and write what you learn.

11. Read *First John 4:1* and write what you learn.

12. Read *Second Peter 2:1-3* and write what you learn about false prophets.

13. From *Second Peter 2:2* define pernicious.

14. From *Second Peter 2:3* define feigned.

15. After defining pernicious and feigned summarize what you learn about false prophets.

16. Read the following scriptures and write what you learn about liars.
    Proverbs 12:22; Revelation 21:8

    _____
    _____
    _____

17. Read ***Second Timothy 2:15*** and tell what your assignment is.

    _____
    _____
    _____
    _____

18. According to ***John 14:26*** what will the Holy Ghost do?

    _____
    _____
    _____
    _____

19. According to ***John 15:26*** the Comforter is also called what?

    _____
    _____
    _____

20. According to ***Luke 11:13*** who will God give the Holy Spirit to?

    _____
    _____
    _____

21. Read ***Proverbs 1:23*** and write what you learn.

    _____
    _____
    _____

22. Read ***Ezekiel 36:27*** and write what you learn.

    _____
    _____
    _____

23. Read *Ephesians 4:14-15* and write what you learn.
_____
_____
_____

24. Read *Proverbs 12:17* and write what your assignment is.
_____
_____
_____

25. Read *Proverbs 12:19* and tell how long truth will last.
_____
_____
_____

26. According to *John 8:32* what will truth do?
_____
_____
_____

27. According to *Ephesians 6:14* what should you have on daily?
_____
_____
_____

EXTRA KNOWLEDGE: The word <u>truth</u> is found 235 times in the Bible. Do a word study and see what God is saying.

Personal Application:

1. Are you a person that tells lies? If so, ask God to deliver you using the scriptures that you have read.

2. How well do you know the Bible? Are you able to recognize someone miss quoting the Bible or using scriptures wrong? If not, what is your plan to increase your knowledge of the Word of God?

CHAPTER 15 ~ VIRTUE

The question was asked, who can find an honorable woman? If the questions has to be asked there is an indication that she is rare or hard to find. A woman that carries herself in such a way that she demands respect when she walks in the room. This type of woman has some standards that she upholds and will not compromise. You may not find her on the cover of many magazines, but she can be found.

What are the characteristics of an honorable woman? She fits the category of one that is righteous. She is not righteous because someone has declared her to be, but she is righteous because God says she is.

As children of God we must conform to the standards of God. He gives us the ability to do them through the power of the Holy Ghost, for we need His help.

As you go over this lesson exam yourself to see where improvements can be made in your life so that you may reflect God.

STUDY QUESTIONS

1. Define virtue.
   _____
   _____
   _____

2. Read *Second Peter 1:3-5* and write what you learn.
   _____
   _____
   _____
   _____

3. According to *Second Peter 1:3* what has God given me?
   _____
   _____
   _____
   _____

4. According to *Second Peter 1:4* what is given to me?
   _____
   _____
   _____
   _____

5. According to *Second Peter 1:5* what should you add to your faith?
   _____
   _____
   _____

6. According to *Philippians 4:8* what should I think on?
   _____
   _____
   _____

7. According to *Titus 2:11-12* what should I deny?

8. According to *Titus 2:11-12* how should I live?

9. Read *Titus 2:11-14* and summarize what you learn.

10. Based on Titus 2:11-14 is virtue a characteristics that should be found in men and women? Explain your answer.

11. According to *Proverbs 12:4* who is a crown to her husband?

12. According to *Proverbs 31:10* whose price is more than rubies and explain what that mean.

13. ***Proverbs 31:10-31*** describes a virtuous woman, take the time to read it, looking up definitions that God may highlight to you and summarize what you learn.

_____

Personal Application:

1. Are you a virtuous person?

2. Do you stand for righteousness?

3. In what area do you need improvement?

CHAPTER 16 ~ WISDOM

When I came to Jesus it was a life changing experience, some things that were exciting to me no longer had my attention, a change had been made in my heart. The following week after my transformation, my husband gave his life to Jesus also. God was so gracious to us by giving us the Holy Ghost {Spirit Baptism}. After our lives was changes a strange thing happened, my husband went backwards or away from Christ. I was a little confused and didn't know what to do. In my prayer time I would always pray for him to come back to Jesus, until one day the Lord showed me I was the problem, a real shocker. How could I be the problem when I was going to church, praying, reading my Bible and doing everything God said to do, or so I thought I was.

God tells us to win people to Him we need wisdom {***Proverb 11:30***} and that a wife could win her husband by her behavior, not her words {***First Corinthians 7:14***}. I did not know how to be the wife that God was talking about and I did not have the wisdom that was necessary to help him make a decision to come back to Jesus. I asked God to help me and he did just that.

The wisdom that God gave me was to schedule my prayer time and Bible reading when he was at work. He taught me how to speak and more importantly when to speak. God began to teach me how to pray for him while he was sleeping. I wish I could tell you that he answered my prayers right away, or within a year, no my sweet reader it took some time, but I can testify that God turned his heart and he submitted himself to the Lord Jesus.

The world has its way of handling things, and God has His ways, I have found that God's way is always better. We need wisdom to make everyday decisions, how to raise our children, how to handle our finances, as well as how to minister to our spouses. The good news is God is willing to give us the necessary help that we need if we ask. As you study this lesson make it your goal to grow in wisdom.

STUDY QUESTIONS

1. Define wisdom.

2. According to *First Corinthians 3:19* the wisdom is this world is what?

3. Read *James 3:13-17* and tell how you will know a wise person.

4. According to *James 3:14-15* list the things that are in one's heart that is consider to cause confusion and every evil work.

5. According to *James 3:17* describe the wisdom that comes from God.

6. Read *First Kings 3:4-15* and write who asked for wisdom and how did God respond. {You can also read *Second Chronicles 1:1-12*}.

7. Read *First Kings 3:28* and write what you learn about the person that was given wisdom from your above answer and how the people responded.
   _____
   _____
   _____

8. Read *First Kings 4:29-34* and tell about Solomon's wisdom.
   _____
   _____
   _____
   _____

9. Read *First Kings 10:1-10* and tell who heard about Solomon's wisdom and what did they do?
   _____
   _____
   _____
   _____

10. Read *First Kings 10:23-24* and tell who did Solomon exceed in wisdom.
    _____
    _____

11. Read *First Kings 10:24* and tell who put the wisdom in Solomon.
    _____
    _____

12. According to *Psalms 37:30* who speaks with wisdom?
    _____
    _____

13. Read the following scriptures and describe how a person receives wisdom.
    James 1:5; Proverbs 1:7, 2:6, 10-11, 6:6, 8:11-22, 35-36; Psalms 90:12
    _____
    _____
    _____
    _____
    _____
    _____

14. Read the following scriptures and describe what wisdom will do for you.
    Proverbs 4:5-13; 24:3, 7

    _____
    _____
    _____
    _____

15. Read the following scriptures and tell why you should stay close to wisdom.
    Proverbs 7:4; Colossians 3:16

    _____
    _____
    _____

16. Read ***Psalms 19:7*** and write what will help you gain wisdom.

    _____
    _____
    _____

17. Read ***Proverbs 1:1-4*** and write why the book of Proverbs was written.

    _____
    _____
    _____
    _____
    _____

18. Read ***Proverbs 1:5*** and describe what a wise person will do.

    _____
    _____
    _____

19. Read ***Proverbs 1:7*** and tell who despised wisdom.

    _____
    _____

20. Define despise from ***Proverbs 1:7*** and summarize what you learn.

    _____
    _____
    _____

21. Read the following scriptures and list some things that will give you wisdom.
    Proverbs 1:5; 8:33; 9:9; 10:8, 14; 11:30; 13:20; 14:16; 18:15; 29:11

    _____
    _____
    _____
    _____
    _____
    _____
    _____
    _____
    _____
    _____
    _____
    _____
    _____
    _____
    _____
    _____

EXTRA KNOWLEDGE: The word <u>wisdom</u> is found 234 times and the word <u>wise</u> is found 247 times in the Bible. Do a word study and see what God is saying.

Personal Application:

1. In what area do you need more wisdom? Making decisions? Parenting?

2. What are you plans to get more wisdom in those areas?

3. Are you able to tell the difference between the wisdom of the world and God's wisdom?

PRAYERS

Areas I am expecting God to mature me.

DATE: _____
SCRIPTURE: _____
CHARACTER: _____
PRAYER: _____
_____
_____
_____
_____
_____

DATE: _____
SCRIPTURE: _____
CHARACTER: _____
PRAYER: _____
_____
_____
_____
_____
_____

DATE: _____
SCRIPTURE: _____
CHARACTER: _____
PRAYER: _____
_____
_____
_____
_____
_____

PRAYERS

Areas I am expecting God to mature me.

DATE: _____
SCRIPTURE: _____
CHARACTER: _____
PRAYER: _____
_____
_____
_____
_____
_____

DATE: _____
SCRIPTURE: _____
CHARACTER: _____
PRAYER: _____
_____
_____
_____
_____
_____

DATE: _____
SCRIPTURE: _____
CHARACTER: _____
PRAYER: _____
_____
_____
_____
_____
_____

EXTRA NOTES

ABOUT THE AUTHOR

Sheila Johnson has been married to her husband Bruce Johnson for 33 years, they have 5 children, {2 have gone on to be with the Lord} and 2 grandchildren. She has served in several areas, Christian Education, Women's Ministry, and Marriage Ministry. She has taught several studies on varies subjects including, "Rebuilding the mind," "Financial stability" and "Manipulation." She is also a preacher of the Gospel of Jesus Christ with some sermons entitled, "Don't quit," and "Know your worth." She and her husband work together to encourage others to be the best version of themselves.

CONTACT INFORMATION:
FACEBOOK: Sheila Johnson
IG: SimplySheilaJohnson
YOUTUBE: Simply Sheila

Made in the USA
Middletown, DE
21 October 2024